THE
ART OF
NAPKIN
FOLDING

Completing the Elegant Table

THE ART OF NAPKIN FOLDING

Completing the Elegant Table

by Susan Kalish

Illustrations by Susan Kalish
Text by Nancy Kalish
Photography by Tony Cenicola

A RUNNING PRESS/FRIEDMAN GROUP BOOK

RUNNING PRESS BOOK PUBLISHERS
PHILADELPHIA, PENNSYLVANIA

A RUNNING PRESS/FRIEDMAN GROUP BOOK

Copyright © 1988 by Michael Friedman Publishing Group, Inc.

9 8 7 6 5 4 3 2

Digit on the right indicates the number of this printing.

Library of Congress Cataloging-in-Publication Data

Kalish, Susan Schoenfeld.
    The art of napkin folding.

    "A Running Press/Friedman Group book"—T.p. verso.
    Includes index.
    1. Napkin folding.   I. Title.
TX879.K33   1988   642'.7   87–42982
ISBN 0-89471-585-2
ISBN 0-89471-398-1 (pbk.)

THE ART OF NAPKIN FOLDING: *Completing the Elegant Table*
was prepared and produced by
Michael Friedman Publishing Group, Inc.
15 West Twenty-sixth Street
New York, New York 10010

Editors: Nancy Kalish and Sharon Kalman
Copy Editor: Mary Forsell
Photo Editor: Philip Hawthorne
Photographer: Tony Cenicola
Production Manager: Karen L. Greenberg

Some napkins provided for photographs by
Party Rentals Ltd., of Teterboro, New Jersey.

Typeset by Lettering Directions Inc.
Color separations by South Seas Graphic Arts Company, Ltd.
Printed and bound in Hong Kong by Leefung-Asco Printers Ltd.

This book may be ordered from the publisher.
Please include $1.50 for postage.
But try your bookstore first.

Running Press Book Publishers
125 South Twenty-second Street
Philadelphia, Pennsylvania 19103

Dedication

To my husband, Howard

Contents

Introduction   *page 8*

Basic Folding Tips   *page 11*

Materials   *page 13*

How to Care for
Your Napkins   *page 15*

Beyond the Basics:
Creative Ideas for
Special Occasions   *page 17*

The Designs
  Envelope Purse   *page 20*
  Pineapple   *page 24*
  Ribboned Roll   *page 26*
  Breakfast Fold   *page 29*
  Basic Napkin Ring Fold   *page 32*
  Bunny   *page 34*
  Bow Tie   *page 37*
  Candle Fold   *page 39*
  Shooting Star   *page 41*

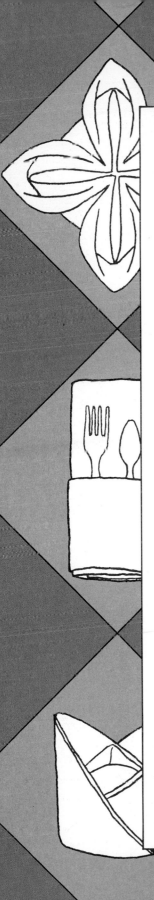

Double Diamond   *page 44*
Roman Column   *page 46*
Pretty Points   *page 49*
Double Roll   *page 51*
Shawl   *page 53*
Ruffle   *page 56*
Triangle Blocks   *page 58*
Peacock's Tail   *page 61*
Deco Fold   *page 64*
Bouquet   *page 67*
Seashell   *page 69*
The Dove   *page 71*
Split Square   *page 73*
Tri-Colored Triangle   *page 75*
Love Knot   *page 78*
Two-Color Picnic Pouch   *page 81*
Carnation   *page 84*
Crown   *page 86*
Lotus   *page 90*
Bishop's Hat   *page 93*
Two-Roll Basket   *page 97*
Buffet Server   *page 102*
Tuxedo Fold   *page 105*
Index *page 110*

BUFFET SERVER

CROWN

RIBBONED ROLL

TWO-ROLL BASKET

INTRODUCTION

Napkins have been folded, pleated, gathered, creased, rolled, stuffed with small surprises, and literally sculpted into dozens of dramatic and intriguing shapes for the last three centuries. They may have begun as unassuming squares of fabric given to upper-class dinner guests who disdained using the tablecloth to wipe their mouths, but today napkins are one of the most inventive and inexpensive ways to wow your family or friends at your next meal or party.

More important, creating a beautiful napkin fold is easy, and even the most complicated fold can be completed in a few minutes. Some take just seconds to do! And although often thought of as a finishing touch, these napkin designs can and should be folded ahead of party time. If they are standing sculptural folds, they can be prefolded and left lying flat until it's time to set the table.

The more than thirty folds in this book can be created in a variety of materials, including heirloom or new linen, cotton, a cotton-and-polyester blend, or that good old standby, paper. Each has a look and feel all its own. Linen looks rich and takes to folds well, a cotton blend has a soft and almost bouncy feel, and paper makes each napkin look like a large origami sculpture. If a fold design works best in a particular material, it is indicated in the instructions for the design.

Keep in mind as well that even the most basic fold can become elegant when created with a beautifully patterned napkin or when folded with two napkins of contrasting colors placed back to back. Take a look at some of our two-napkin designs, such as Two-Color Picnic Pouch or the Love Knot, which uses four different napkins to create a gorgeous and useful trivet for a new twist on napkin folding.

It's fun and practical to have a variety of napkins of different patterns, colors, and materials on hand. Collecting accessories such as napkin rings and holders is also useful. Whichever type of napkin you choose, however, you'll find you'll get excellent folding results with a minimum of practice.

Keep in mind that napkin folding is not a precise art that has to be done picture perfect; you'll probably be able to successfully complete most of the folds in this book the very first time you try them. To keep track of what folds you've been creating, however, it's a good idea to buy a package of white paper napkins and fold each in a different design. Label each design and keep them completely folded inside a shoe box. Then take them out the next time you are planning a party. This will make it easier to choose one or two to fold because you'll know which you've mastered and look the most marvelous on your table.

BASIC FOLDING TIPS

The instructions for each design in this book begin with the napkin open and placed flat on the table before you. If you are instructed to fold "down" into a rectangle or other shape, it means that you should lift the edge of the napkin farthest away from you and fold it "down" to meet the edge closest to you. Do the opposite if you are instructed to fold "up." Another vital tip to remember, however obvious it seems, is that the instructions for folding should be followed precisely. For example, the phrase "top edge" indicates a different location from "top point"; the former refers to the edge of the napkin farthest away from you, while the latter indicates the angle farthest away from you.

In general, the more steps a folded design has, the bigger the napkin should be to avoid a too-tiny result. Many of these designs can be folded with napkins as small as 17 inches (42.5 centimeters) square. Napkins that are at least 20 inches (50 centimeters) square usually produce the best results, however.

Napkins should be laundered (and starched, if necessary) and ironed before being put away so that they are ready to fold. If possible, store all napkins, especially those of linen or damask, flat in a stack so that they don't develop any extra creases.

If your cotton or linen napkins are not creasing as sharply as you desire, use a little spray starch and reiron them briefly. Take care not to overdo the spray starch, however, or the napkin may scorch.

Do all your folding on a clean, flat surface such as your dining room table before it has been set. Wherever you fold, don't do it by holding the napkin up in front of you in the air! It's the surest way to create strange angles and sloppy corners. Keep your napkin on the table.

When folding a design for the first time with an ironed linen or cotton napkin, it's best to practice with paper first to avoid extra creases.

If you are creating these designs in either linen or cotton (rather than paper or a cotton-polyester blend), begin with a pressed napkin. Unless indicated, however, do not press any of the finished folds in place. This tends to give the design a stiff, old-fashioned look. The napkin folds in this book look better when creased softly.

All napkins should be square or nearly square to fold well. Be sure to take this into account when buying napkins, especially paper or vintage ones.

The designs in this book can be created with a variety of materials—paper, cotton, cotton-polyester blend, and linen. The only fabric that will simply not work is one-hundred-percent polyester, which won't absorb food or liquids easily and is too bouncy to stay in place. Designs folded with one-hundred-percent polyester napkins will often gradually unfold themselves before the dinner guests arrive.

Fold all your napkins before beginning to prepare the food for a large dinner party or buffet, while you are still calm. This way, you have plenty of time to fold. The folding itself can be an especially relaxing activity, perfect for curing pre-party jitters. Even napkins that stand up on the table can be folded ahead of time. Just leave them flat in a stack, and stand them up at the last minute. Make sure to store folded napkins far away from the kitchen to avoid spills and stains.

Some designs—such as the Roman Column and Breakfast Fold—call for a napkin holder or glass as support. If this is the case, make sure that the holder or glass not only looks good, but also holds the napkin the way it should before you decide to present that fold at a dinner party.

Where exactly to place your napkin design on the table is up to you. Many designs look best standing up on or lying across the dinner plate. Others should be stood up in glasses. Still others look best placed beyond the plate or to its left. Suggestions for placement can be found in the photographs and in the instructions for each design. But napkin folding and table setting are arts, not sciences with specific rules. In the end, the finishing touches are up to you.

Materials

Paper

Most of the designs in this book look marvelous in paper, which gives them a sleek, sculptural look with a crisp edge. Paper is, of course, the cheapest and easiest material to fold because it takes creases and holds its shape so easily. This makes it ideal for those designs that stand up on the table.

Keep in mind, however, that paper is also the most fragile of folding materials. Most paper napkins are only one-ply thick. It's worth the time, therefore, to seek out three-ply paper napkins if possible. If you can't find them and your designs are not holding their shapes well, try using two napkins together for extra body. Two contrasting colors look especially nice.

A wide variety of high-quality paper napkins can be found at party-supply stores. They are available in both cocktail and dinner sizes, but always use the latter for folding. Remember to buy only square or nearly square paper napkins, because those are the only kind that can be used for the designs in this book. Also, keep in mind that solid-colored paper napkins are usually better for folding since those with patterns are printed only on the square facing the front of the package. Also use care when folding to make sure the unprinted side faces inward on the finished design.

Cotton, Linen, and Lace

Many of us are fortunate enough to have inherited lovely linen or cotton napkins, some of which may have decorative edges or hand embroidery. Many of these heirlooms are not true squares, but that doesn't mean they can't be folded beautifully anyway.

Try such designs as the Crown, Peacock's Tail, and Buffet Server, which will fold nicely with napkins like these because the first step is to fold the napkin into a rectangle. This way, only the edges, and not the corners, have to be even. Or use your heirlooms to add rich elegance to more free-flowing designs such as Shooting Star.

Linen and cotton fold best when lightly starched and pressed. Remember to not use too much starch, however, or you may scorch your napkin. Store washed and ironed napkins flat in a stack so that they are ready for folding. And practice new designs with paper so as not to add too many creases.

If you enjoy folding with linen or cotton, buy a package of inexpensive paper napkins and fold each in a different design. Label them and keep them folded in a shoe box as a reference for your dinner parties.

Many people love the look of a delicate lace napkin over a solid color "liner." The two can be folded together and look gorgeous in many of the designs in this book, including the Ribboned Roll or Bouquet. If your lace napkins are especially old or fragile, however, you might consider collecting them from your guests after the first course to avoid undue wear, tear, and staining.

Many cotton or linen napkins are hemmed on two sides. If this is the case with yours, before beginning to fold, place the napkin so that the hemmed edges are at the top and bottom rather than at the sides so that the napkin will fold better.

Your fine fabric napkin will also fold better if the selvage is going the right way. Heirloom cotton or linen napkins are usually hemmed on two sides. The other two are plain, or "finished." These edges are the selvages. Begin folding with the selvages running vertically. This will help the napkin hold its shape well.

Finally, there are several spectacular designs in this book, such as the Pretty Points, that was especially created to show off your napkins with monograms or scalloped edges in a truly elegant manner. At the other extreme, there are several folds, such as the Double Roll and Seashell that look fabulous when done with a napkin with a loose and rather rustic weave. Keep in mind, however, that such loosely woven napkins may produce a bulkier result.

How To Care For Your Napkins

One definition of good hosts and hostesses might be those people who can present their best china, crystal, and linen to guests and not worry about breakage or stains.

While your dishes probably won't be broken with regularity, few tablecloths or napkins get through an entire dinner party unscathed. After all, they are there not only for decoration, but also for guests to use. Therefore, either resign yourself to a few stains or keep your linens in the closet and use paper.

The good news is that many of these stains can be removed successfully, even if they have dried. The only type of napkin that it's probably best not to treat yourself is one that has to be dry-cleaned. The most you should do is sprinkle a fresh liquid stain with either cornstarch or a little salt and leave it on until the liquid is absorbed. Do not rub or you may damage the grain of the fabric and create nubs. If you must rub, do it very, very gently. Make sure you tell the dry cleaner what the stain is if you know.

Concerning washable napkins, a common stain such as wine, for example, should be sponged with cold water if fresh or soaked in cold water with a heavy dose of white vinegar or white wine added. Then wash in warm water with a mild detergent. The same should be done for soda stains or those made by berries or other fruits.

For stains caused by catsup, tomatoes, or vegetables, soak the napkins in warm water with mild detergent, then launder in the normal manner. This is also the rule for lipstick or other cosmetic stains.

Soak the napkin in cold water with detergent if the stain has been made by a protein such as egg, meat, or even gravy. If this doesn't work completely, sponge on a bit of cleaning fluid. Allow to dry, then launder. This method also works with mustard.

Simply soak dairy stains such as milk or ice cream in cold water; then launder.

After a romantic dinner for two, you may find that candle wax has dripped onto your napkins. Scrape it off gently with a blunt knife, then place paper towels under and over the napkin and iron it until the towels have absorbed all the wax. Change the towel if it becomes saturated. When all the wax has been absorbed, launder the napkin normally.

Finally, if you accidentally scorch your napkin while ironing it, immediately sponge it with ammonia or hydrogen peroxide. Then rinse it well and launder.

Not all these techniques work for all napkins, so use your judgment, especially when it comes to antiques or heirlooms. The most stain-resistant types are the cotton-polyester-blend napkins. In addition, you may want to spray some napkins with a stain-resistor such as Scotch Guard, but be aware that such a spray may make the napkin so impervious to liquids and foods that it becomes useless to your dinner guest.

Beyond the Basics: Creative Ideas for Special Occasions

Even the smallest touch can make a napkin fold even more special. It might be a beautiful ribbon tied around the napkin in place of an ordinary napkin ring, or a piece of twine to create a rustic feel, perfect for a picnic. The following are some more tips for turning even the plainest napkin into something that will draw oohs and ahs from your guests.

If you're having more than two people at your table, fold the napkins in two different designs and place them at alternate settings. Or fold each napkin a different way to create a "charm-bracelet" effect.

For extra fun at a child's party, fold white- or light-colored paper napkins in whimsical shapes, such as the Bunny, and provide a variety of crayons with which to color in the features. Or, fold very large yellow paper napkins into the Crown design and write each child's name on the brim.

Many things can be placed inside a napkin fold, including rolls, mints, cutlery, or small party favors. Among the folds suitable for tucking extras inside are the Two-Color Picnic Pouch and Triangle Blocks. Or tuck a place card or small blossom into one of the exposed folds for a truly elegant look for a formal dinner party. The Tuxedo Fold as well as the Bishop's Hat will work splendidly.

Some of the more sculptural folds such as the Lotus, Tricolored Triangle, Love Knot, and Two-Roll Basket are grand enough to use as a centerpiece as long as they are folded with very large napkins. You might create several of the same design to place at intervals on a long table or alternate a few different designs for added intrigue.

You don't have to have inherited monogrammed napkins in order to enjoy that richly elegant look. You can embroider your own initials on your napkins with the help of a book on monogram embroidery. Simply follow the instructions, keeping the size of the embroidery in proportion with the rest of the napkin. Although this does take a bit of time and effort, it's an inexpensive endeavor, and the resulting look is pretty enough to create an heirloom worthy of being passed on.

THE DESIGNS

Envelope Purse

This elegant "purse" will look lovely draped across a plate. Surprise your guests with a small sweet treat or savory tidbit tucked inside.

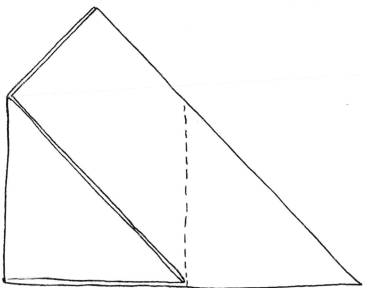

1. Fold the napkin up into a triangle with the point facing up.

2. Starting on the left side, fold the napkin into thirds along the bottom edge as shown in this diagram and the next.

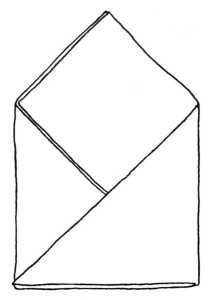

3. Repeat with the right side.

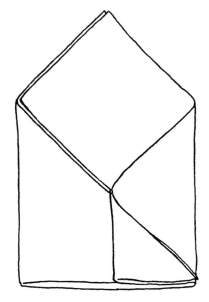

4. Fold the first layer of the new bottom left corner back to meet the new bottom right corner.

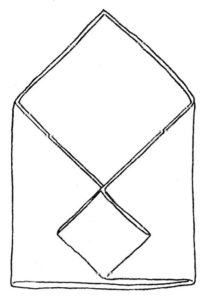

5. Pick up the point of the first layer of the bottom right corner, and lift it to the left and up to meet the place where the two sides come together. This will form a small diamond. Make minor adjustments, if necessary.

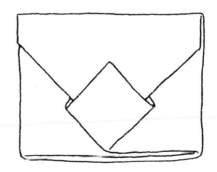

6. Bring the top point of the napkin down, and tuck it all the way into the small diamond. Lay the napkin flat on a plate.

Pineapple

This frilly fold can look like a pineapple or a fan, depending on which end faces the diner. Either way, it is simple yet elegant.

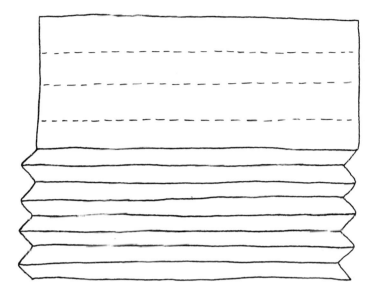

1. Grasp both bottom corners of the napkin and pleat it tightly, accordion style. Pleat from the bottom up, and do not let go of the corners at any time.

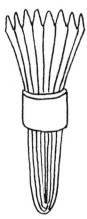

2. When you reach the top edge, bring the two short ends together in one quick motion. Holding all the pleats in place, pull the closed end through a napkin ring to within 3 inches (7.5 centimeters) of the open edges.

Ribboned Roll

Because of its resemblance to a diploma, this fold is a natural for a graduation party. Use a crisp, white linen napkin tied with a bright red ribbon.

1. Fold the top edge of the napkin to meet the bottom edge to form a rectangle with the closed edge on the top.

2. Fold the top right and bottom right corners in to meet in the center to form a small triangle pointing right.

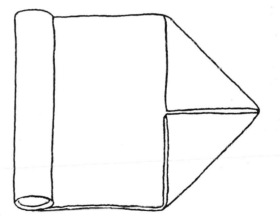

3. Loosely roll the napkin all the way from left to right.

4. Tie it in the center with a piece of ribbon, finished off with a bow.

RIBBONED ROLL

BREAKFAST FOLD

Breakfast Fold

A particularly sprightly sight, this napkin makes a wonderful accent on a tray alongside the morning meal. Use a cotton-polyester blend napkin that is easy to clean should a drop of coffee or juice fall on it.

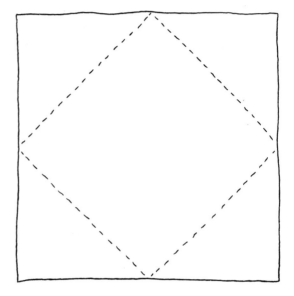

1. Place the napkin in a square before you.

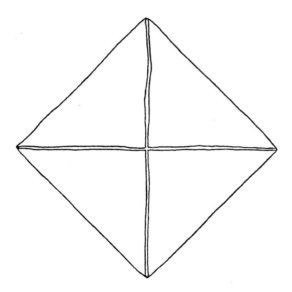

2. Fold all four corners in to meet at the center.

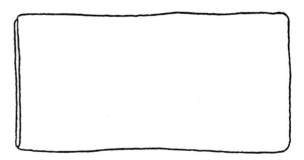

3. Shift the napkin so that it is in a square before you once more. Bring the bottom edge up to meet the top edge.

1. Bring the left edge over to meet the right edge.

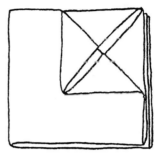

5. Fold the top layer of the right corner a little bit past the center point of the napkin.

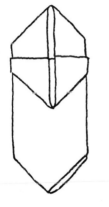

6. Shift the napkin so it is in a diamond shape before you. Then fold back the two side points, overlapping them behind the napkin.

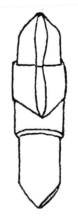

7. Pressing the sides back, slip the napkin into a napkin ring. Lay the napkin on or beside a plate with the top pointing away from the diner.

Basic Napkin Ring Fold

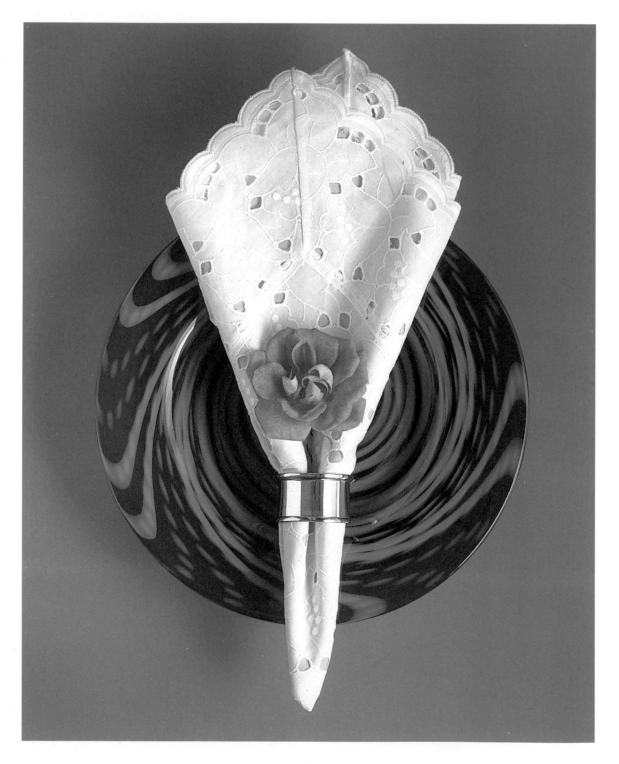

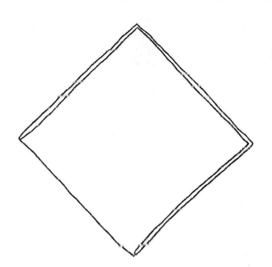

This design is excellent practice for beginners and is guaranteed to look perfect the very first time it is attempted. It can be created with any type of napkin.

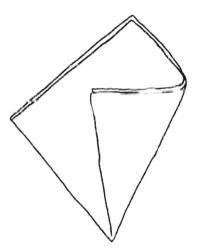

1. Fold the napkin into quarters, and place it in a diamond shape before you with the folded corner pointing toward the bottom.

2. Fold the napkin into thirds, beginning by bringing the right point toward the upper edge until a sharp point is formed on the bottom edge of the napkin.

3. Fold the left side in the same manner to meet the new right edge. The bottom corner should be at a sharp angle.

4. Turn the napkin over, and gently squeeze the right and left edges forward and together as much as necessary at the bottom with one hand. With the other hand, slip a napkin ring over the bottom point and up to almost the center of the napkin. Place on a plate or beside it.

Bunny

This design is a delightful addition to a child's party. If you fold it using a plain white paper napkin, the kids can use crayons to fill in the rabbit's features.

1. Fold the napkin up into a triangle.

2. Grasp the bottom edge, and fold it up one quarter of the way to the top point.

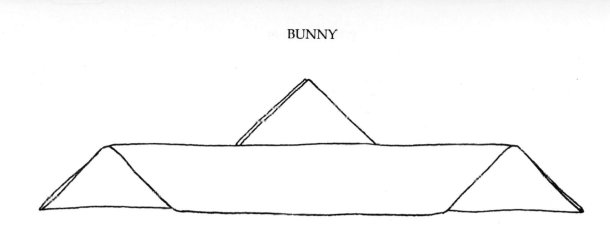

3. Fold this edge up the same amount once again.

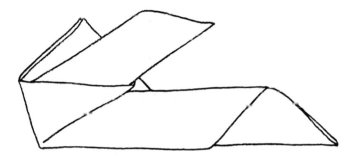

4. Bring the bottom left corner up and across the napkin at a diagonal so that it crosses the right edge about two-thirds from the bottom.

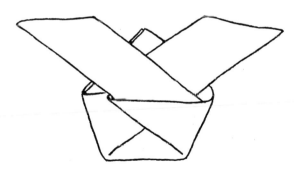

5. Repeat with the bottom right corner.

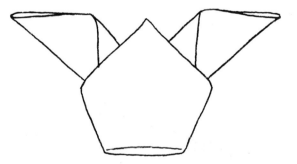

6. Turn the napkin over and place it on a plate so that the "bunny's ears" are pointing upwards.

BUNNY

BOW TIE

Bow Tie

Use this simple but fancy fold at your next formal dinner party. The bow-tie effect is most striking when created with either white or black napkins. Or try alternating the two if you want to truly dazzle your guests.

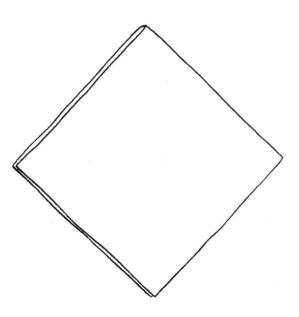

1. Fold the napkin into quarters and place in a diamond shape before you with the open point at the left.

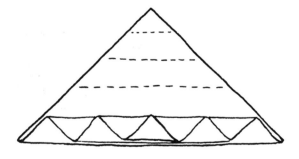

2. Pleat it completely from the bottom up, accordion style.

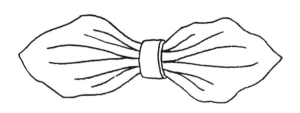

3. Holding the folds in place, insert the napkin into a napkin ring, so that the ring is at the center. Fan out the folds, and center the napkin on a plate in a bow-tie shape.

Candle Fold

With a distinct resemblance to a candelabrum, this fold is an easy way to add an elegant touch to your table. Be sure to use an unstarched napkin.

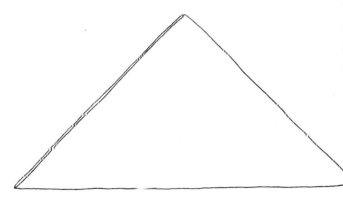

1. Fold the napkin into a triangle with the point facing up.

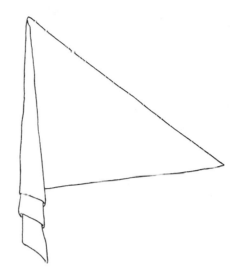

2. Holding your finger at the top point, grasp the left corner and pull the left edge of the triangle taut. Still holding the napkin in this manner, roll the left edge toward the center five or six times. Weigh it down.

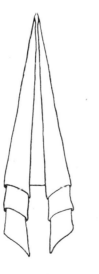

3. Repeat the procedure with the right edge. Add extra rolls on both sides if necessary to bring the two rolls to within 1 inch (2.5 centimeters) apart along the bottom edge.

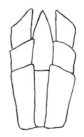

4. Fold the top half of the napkin back and away from you. Place it on the plate so that the points face away from the diner.

CANDLE FOLD

SHOOTING STAR

Shooting Star

Especially appealing when created with a boldly colored napkin, this design seems about to burst forth from its holder. It works best with a soft and bouncy napkin made of a cotton-polyester blend.

1. Fold the napkin down into a triangle.

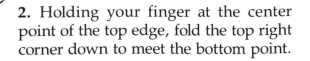

2. Holding your finger at the center point of the top edge, fold the top right corner down to meet the bottom point.

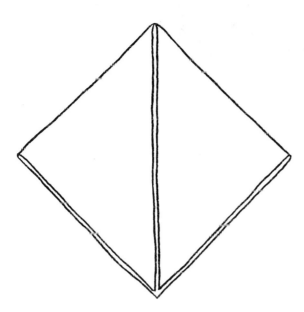

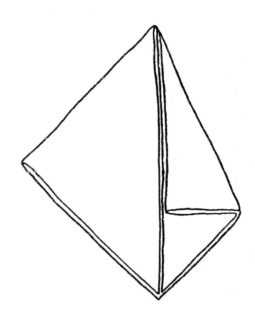

3. Repeat with the top left corner.

4. Still holding your finger at the top point, pick up the right corner, and bring it to meet the center line of the diamond to form a right angle. Repeat with the left corner.

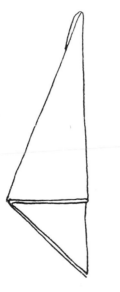

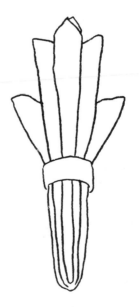

5. Fold the napkin back and away from you along the vertical center line. Turn napkin upside down.

6. Holding the folds together with one hand, slip the slimmer point of the napkin through a napkin ring. Arrange the loose folds nicely.

Double Diamond

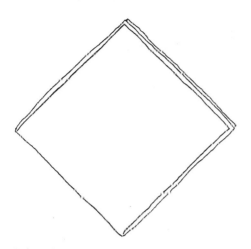

This neat geometric fold looks best in bright colors as part of modern table settings. It can be created with any large napkin.

1. Fold the napkin into quarters and place it in a diamond shape before you so that the open corner points up.

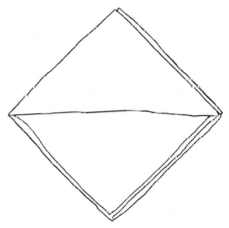

2. Fold the first layer of the top point down to meet the bottom point.

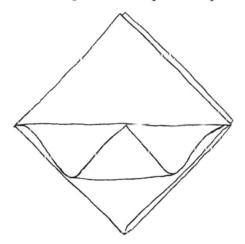

3. Fold that same point up to meet the center line.

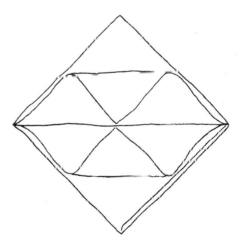

4. Fold the second layer of the top point down to meet the center line.

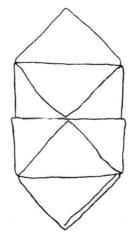

5. Fold the side points back and away from you so that they overlap in the back, and lay the finished napkin flat on the dinner plate.

Roman Column

Though it looks like a piece of an ancient temple, this sleek fold complements modern table settings best. It can be dressed up for a formal dinner with a fancy napkin ring.

1. Fold the napkin in half to form a triangle with the point facing down, toward you.

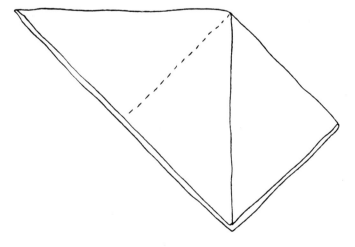

2. Holding your finger at the center point of the fold along the top, fold the right corner down to the bottom point.

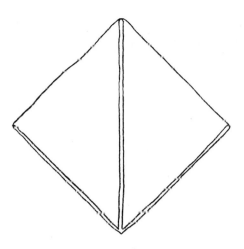

3. Repeat with the left corner. Turn the napkin over. The top point should be closed in the fold; the bottom point should be open.

4. Fold the left and right corners to meet in the center.

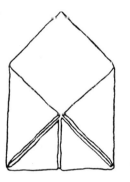

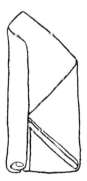

5. Fold the bottom corner up to meet the center point as well.

6. Roll the left long side of the napkin twice or more to the center point.

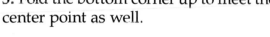

7. Repeat with the right side.

8. Holding both rolls in place, insert the flat end of the napkin into a napkin holder so that the point sticks straight up. Stand up the napkin roll either on the plate or by its side.

ROMAN COLUMN

PRETTY POINTS

Pretty Points

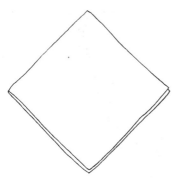

1. Fold the napkin into quarters, and place it in a diamond shape before you so that the closed corner points up.

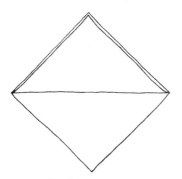

2. Starting at the bottom point, take the first layer of napkin and bring it up to meet the top point.

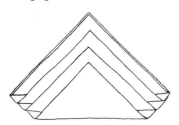

3. Then bring the second layer of the bottom point to within 0.5 to 1 inch (1.25 to 2.5 centimeters) of the top point. Repeat with remaining two layers, placing each layer a little further down, so that each edge shows and they are all spaced evenly apart. Place the napkin flat on the dinner plate with the triangles pointing to the left of the diner.

While pretty when folded with a plain napkin, this design was created to show off those lovely linen or cotton heirlooms with scalloped edges.

Variation

Repeat steps 1 through 3.

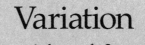

4. Turn the napkin over.

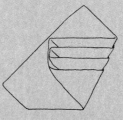

5. Fold the right side of the napkin over so that it is a little bit past the center and the four edges are lying horizontally. Fold the other side over in the same manner.

6. Turn the napkin over. Fold the sides back a bit, fold the bottom edge up 1 inch (2.5 centimeters), and place the bottom edge in a napkin ring so that the napkin stands up.

Double Roll

This fold is easy enough to create quickly when you want something pretty to add to the breakfast tray or the luncheon table. Its soft look is best achieved with a cotton-polyester blend cloth.

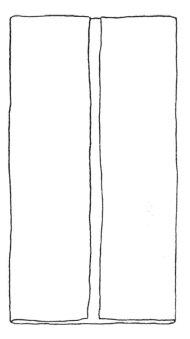

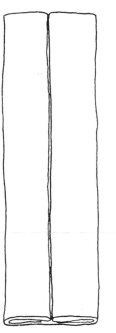

1. With the napkin lying flat, fold the two sides toward the center, leaving a 1-inch (2.5-centimeter) gap between the two edges.

2. Fold the new outer edges so that they meet in the center.

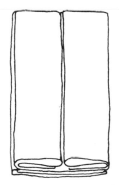

3. Fold the top of the rectangle in half horizontally and away from you, so that the two sides of the folded napkin are identical. Lay the napkin flat on the plate with the open end of the rolls facing the diner, or place it beside the plate in the same manner.

DOUBLE ROLL

SHAWL

Shawl

This intricate fold will add an oriental accent to your tablesetting. Be sure to use a starched cotton or linen napkin that holds the creases well.

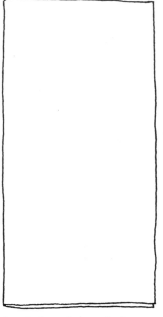

1. Fold the left edge of the napkin to meet the right so that a rectangle is formed with a closed fold on the left.

2. Fold the top edge down about 1 inch (2.5 centimeters) on the back side of the napkin.

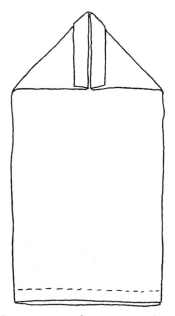

3. Holding your finger at the center point of the top edge, bring the left and right corners toward the center to form a triangle.

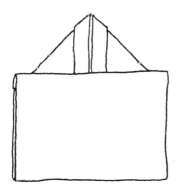

4. Fold the bottom edge up about 1 inch on the front side of the napkin. Then bring that same edge up to overlap the bottom of the triangle by 1 inch.

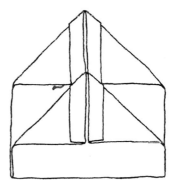

5. Holding your finger at the center point of the top edge again, bring the top right and left corners down to meet in the center and form another triangle below the first.

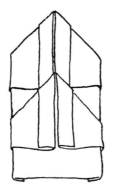

6. Fold the right and left edges so that they meet or almost meet on the back side of the napkin.

Ruffle

This breezy design is perfect for a spring or summer lunch. Any kind of napkin will do, but this fold looks particularly perky when created with a striped one.

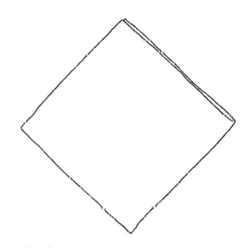

1. Fold the napkin into quarters, and place it in a diamond shape before you with the open corner pointing up.

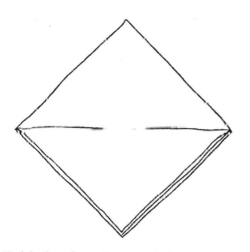

2. Fold the first layer of the top point down to meet the bottom point.

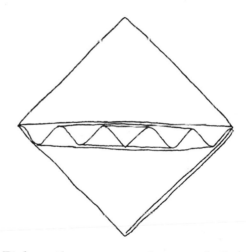

3. Pick up that same top layer and pleat it four times, accordion style. Weigh the closed pleats down with a glass.

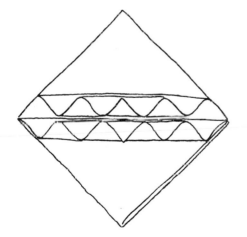

4. Pick up the second layer of the top point, and pleat it in the same manner, folding it at the same intervals to form a symmetrical pattern. Line up the new band of closed pleats right above and next to the first. Weigh this down as well.

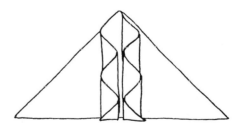

5. Holding the center points of the pleats down firmly, fold the right half of the napkin back and away from you to meet the left half.

Triangle Blocks

For your next buffet lunch or dinner, try folding napkins in this style using a variety of colors. This fold is easy to stack and looks especially attractive when layered. For an extra treat, try folding a mint or other small sweet inside.

1. Place the napkin in a square before you. Fold down the top edge, and fold up the bottom edge so that they meet in the center.

2. Fold the top edge down to meet the bottom edge.

3. Holding your finger at the top right corner, bring the bottom right corner up to meet an imaginary horizontal center line. If you wish to fold in a small wrapped mint or other sweet, tuck it under this last fold now, and continue the folding process.

4. Holding your finger at the new bottom right corner, bring the top right corner down to meet the bottom edge. This should create an equilateral triangle.

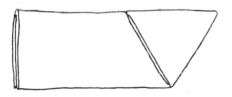

5. Bring the bottom right corner up to meet the top edge. Fold the napkin twice more in this manner to create a folded triangle.

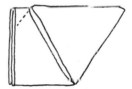

6. Fold the top left corner down a tiny bit, and fold the rectangle on the left to the right. Tuck it all the way into the flap created by the fold. This should even out the edge of the napkin.

7. Stack several of these napkins on top of one another like blocks.

TRIANGLE BLOCKS

PEACOCK'S TAIL

Peacock's Tail

Delicately spread across a plate of fine china, this fold really does resemble a peacock's frothy tail. Placed beside the plate, it takes on an abstract but still beautiful appearance. Fold this design for your most special parties.

1. Fold the napkin down into a rectangle. The folded edge should be along the top.

2. Fold the right edge to meet the left edge to form a square.

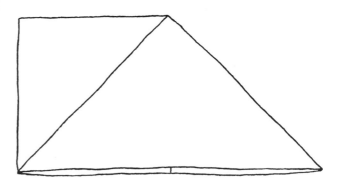

3. Grasping the top layer of the bottom left corner, pull it gently and directly to the right, past the right edge to form a large triangle pointing upward. Make small adjustments if necessary.

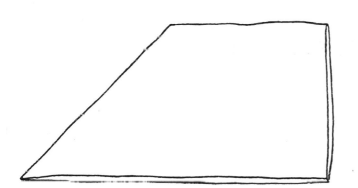

4. Turn the napkin over.

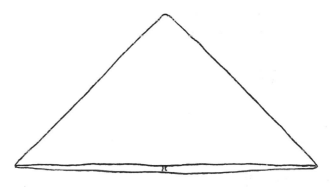

5. Grasping the top layer of the bottom right corner, pull it gently and directly to the left to meet the bottom left corner. This will create one large triangle.

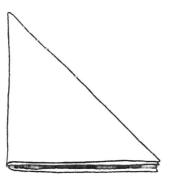

6. Bring the bottom left corner to meet the bottom right corner. You should now have four folded triangles.

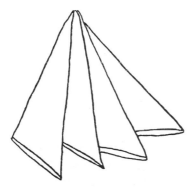

7. Hold the folds together at the top point, and fan out the four triangles with your other hand by grasping the top three and moving them a bit to the left. Repeat with the top two, and finally with the remaining triangle, trying to space them evenly apart. Place this design on the plate with the folds pointing up, as shown in the photograph, so that it looks like a bird.

Deco Fold

This elegant fold resembles an art deco lamp. Make sure you use a large napkin measuring at least 20 × 20 inches (50 by 50 centimeters) that holds a crease well.

1. Place the napkin in a square before you.

2. Fold the four corners of the napkin to meet in the center, and shift the napkin so that it is in a square before you once again.

3. Fold the top edge down to meet the bottom edge.

 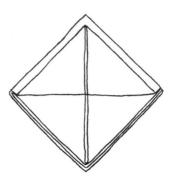

4. Fold the left edge to meet the right edge, and rotate the napkin so that the open point is facing down.

5. Bring the top layer of the bottom point up to within 0.5 inch (1.25 centimeters) of the top point.

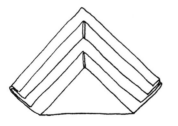 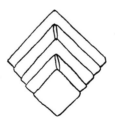

6. Repeat with remaining three layers, placing each layer a little further down, so that each edge shows and they are all spaced evenly apart.

7. Fold both side edges back at a sharp angle to create a point at the bottom.

Bouquet

This design will remind your guests of a bouquet of wild flowers when it is tied with a piece of twine. Use a napkin ring or a length of ribbon, however, for more stylish results.

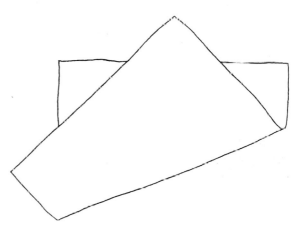

1. With the napkin lying flat before you, bring the bottom right corner up to and beyond the center point of the top edge, forming two equal triangles on either side of the edge.

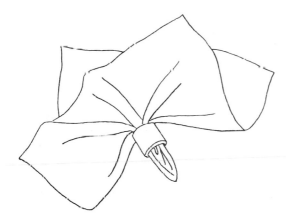

2. Place the napkin ring on its side at the center point of the diagonal bottom edge, and reach through it with your thumb and forefinger to grasp the napkin. Loosely draw the napkin through the ring, gathering it in loose folds, about halfway up its length.

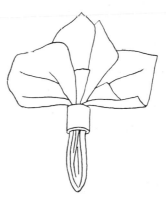

3. Shake the napkin if necessary to make the folds fall attractively. Place the napkin on the plate so that the "bouquet" points upward.

BOUQUET

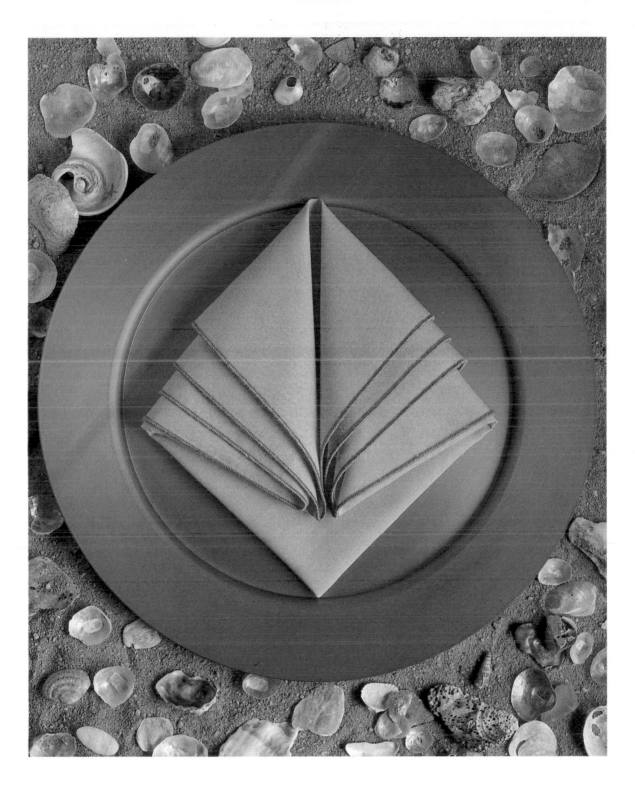

SEASHELL

Seashell

The folds of this napkin gently rise up to form contours similar to those of a shell. This lovely shape, best folded in a cotton-polyester blend, is suitable for either casual or formal meals.

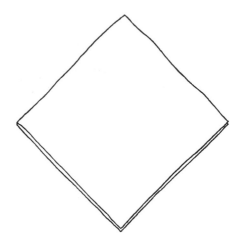

1. Fold the napkin into quarters, and place it in a diamond shape before you so that the closed corner points up.

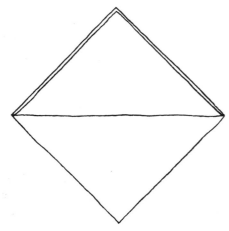

2. Starting at the bottom point, pick up the first layer of napkin, and bring it up to meet the top point.

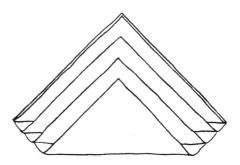

3. Bring the second layer of the bottom point to within 0.5 to 1 inch (1.25 to 2.5 centimeters) of the top point. Repeat with remaining two layers, placing each layer a little further down, so that each edge shows and the they are all spaced evenly apart.

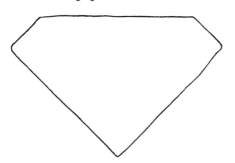

4. Flip the napkin over. The point should now be facing down.

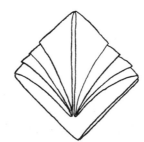

5. Holding your finger at the center point of the top edge, bring the top right and left corners down to meet in the middle and create a point at the top. Pinch the folds together at the bottom and top, and fluff them up a bit before placing the napkin on a plate.

The Dove

This design is a good fold for beginners. The end result will hold its shape more easily if you use a heavy cotton napkin.

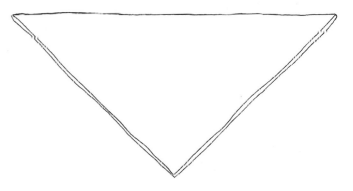

1. Fold the napkin in half to form a triangle with the point facing down, toward you. Make sure the corners are even.

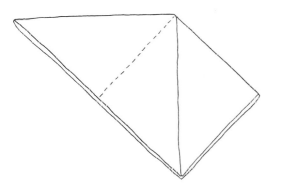

2. Holding your finger at the center point of the top fold, fold the right corner down to the bottom point.

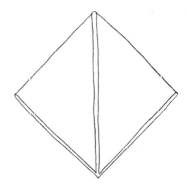

3. Repeat with the left corner.

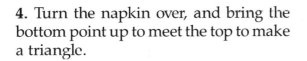

4. Turn the napkin over, and bring the bottom point up to meet the top to make a triangle.

5. Lift the napkin up at the center of the bottom, and stand the napkin up, facing away from the diner.

THE DOVE

SPLIT SQUARE

Split Square

Use a starched napkin for this sleek geometric design, which looks especially striking when framed by a boldly colored round plate.

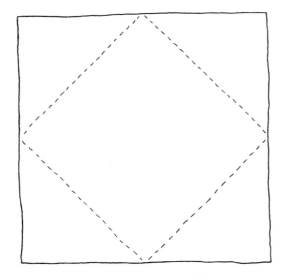

1. If the napkin has a right side and a wrong side, turn it wrong side up, and lay it flat down so that it is in a square shape before you.

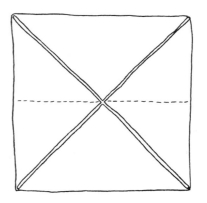

2. Fold the four corners in so that the points meet in the center. Adjust the napkin carefully so that all the new corners are sharp. Rotate the napkin so that it again forms a square.

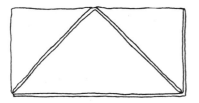

3. Grasping the center point of the right edge with one hand and the left edge with the other, pick the napkin up slightly, and fold it back in half horizontally. You should now have a rectangle with the closed edge along the top.

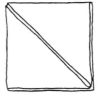

4. Fold the new right edge to meet the left edge.

Tri-Colored Triangle

This geometric design is most striking when folded with three different colored napkins of equal size. Perfect for a meal of three courses, this fold only looks complicated.

1. Bring the top edge of the first napkin (A) down to meet the bottom edge.

2. Fold the new top and bottom edges so that they meet in the center.

3. Then fold the bottom edge up to meet the top edge. Repeat steps 1 through 3 with the two other napkins (B and C).

4. Fold the short right edge of napkin A to meet the left edge.

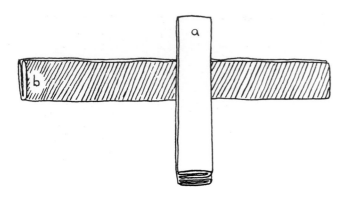

5. Lay napkin B down with the long edges running horizontally. Place napkin A vertically on top of napkin B, as shown in the diagram.

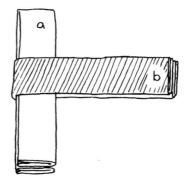

6. Fold the left side of napkin B to meet the right side. Adjust napkin A so that it extends farther below napkin B, leaving a square of napkin A above it.

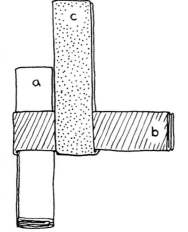

7. Place the center of napkin C along the bottom edge of napkin B and flush with napkin A, and bring the two short ends up and around napkin B.

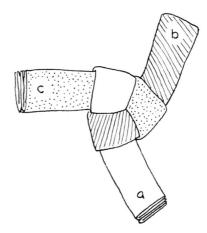

8. Tuck the two ends of napkin C into and through the middle fold of the top square of napkin A. Gently pull on the three ends to create a tricolored triangle in the middle.

TRI-COLORED TRIANGLE

Love Knot

Both decorative and useful, this design can be folded in a snap when you need a beautiful extra trivet for a family meal or dinner party. It looks most striking when folded with four equal-sized napkins of different colors.

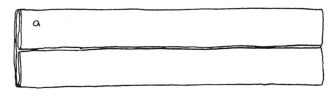

1. Bring the top edge of napkin A down to meet the bottom edge.

2. Fold the new top and bottom edges so that they meet in the center.

3. Then fold the bottom edge up to meet the top edge. Repeat steps 1 through 3 with napkins B, C, and D.

4. Fold the short right edge of napkin A to meet the left edge.

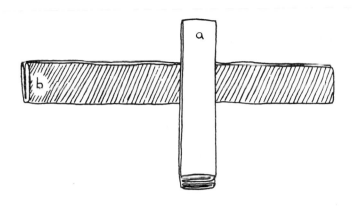

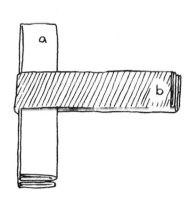

5. Lay napkin B down with the long edges running horizontally. Place napkin A vertically on top of napkin B, as shown in the diagram.

6. Fold the right side of napkin B to meet the left side. Adjust napkin A so there is more on the side below napkin B and a square of napkin A above it.

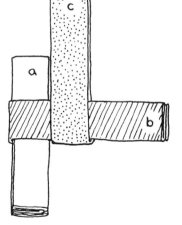

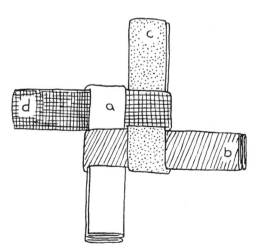

7. Place the center of napkin C along the bottom edge of napkin B and flush with napkin A, and bring the two short ends up and around napkin B.

8. Place the center of napkin D on the edge of napkin C directly above where it meets napkin B, and bring the two short ends up and pull them through the opening made by napkin A. Pull gently on all four ends of the napkins to create a multicolored square in the middle.

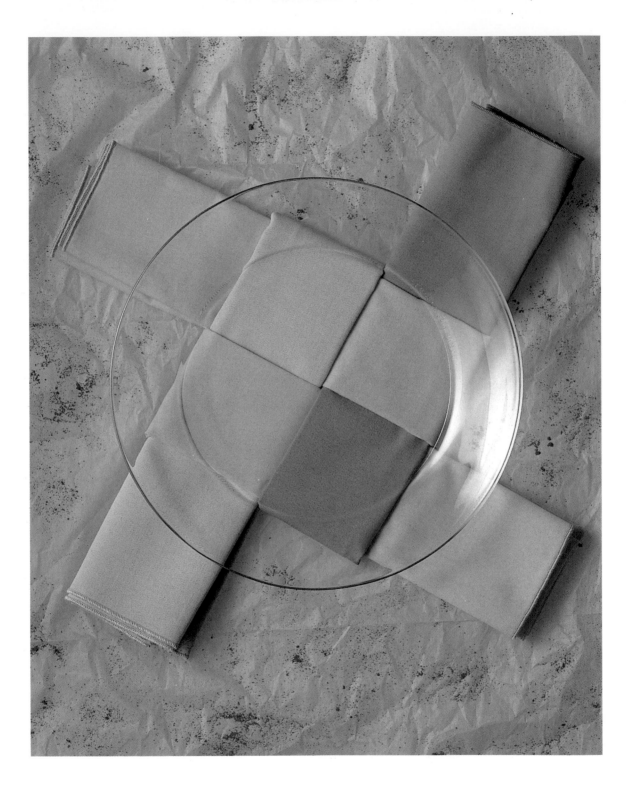

LOVE KNOT

TWO-COLOR PICNIC POUCH

Two-Color Picnic Pouch

Here's an easy and colorful way to carry place settings to a picnic. Each pouch contains the necessary silverware and two napkins, especially handy when eating an alfresco meal. You will need two large napkins of contrasting colors and equal size.

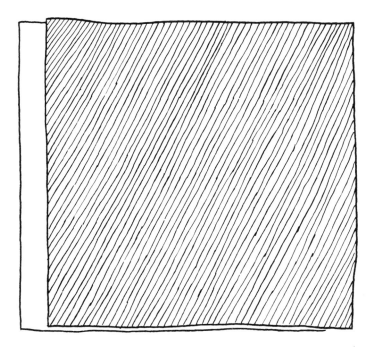

1. Place the napkins on top of each other, staggering the right and left edges to create a 2-inch (5-centimeter) stripe of one color on the left side.

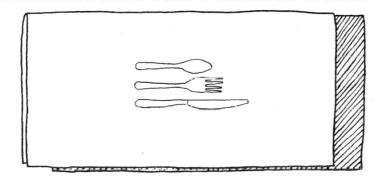

2. Fold both napkins down together to create a rectangle with the closed edge along the top. Place up to three pieces of silverware in the center of the napkin and pointing toward the stripe.

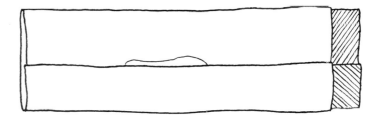

3. Fold the bottom edge of the napkin up to the center.

4. Fold the top edge down to almost meet the bottom edge.

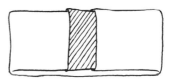

5. Fold the left edge to the center, or as close to it as the silverware will allow. Fold the right edge toward the center as well, and tuck the left edge under the first two layers of the stripe.

Carnation

This pretty fold, reminiscent of a pin-wheel, is perfect for a lighthearted lunch or supper. Choose a patterned ribbon to hold it together with some character.

1. Fold the top and bottom edges in so that they meet in the center.

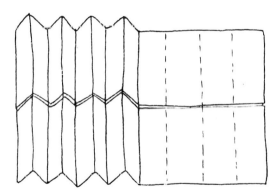

2. Pleat the napkin accordion style, beginning at the left side.

3. Holding the pleats together, stand the napkin up on its edge, and tie a small bow around the center point with a piece of ribbon.

4. Fan the pleats out into a circle, and place the napkin flat on a plate.

Crown

Guests will be amused by this royal design, and children may have to be told to keep this napkin on their laps, not their heads. Since this fold stands up, it's best to create it with a heavy cotton or linen napkin. It also works well with paper.

1. Fold the napkin upward to form a rectangle. The folded edge should be on the bottom, facing you.

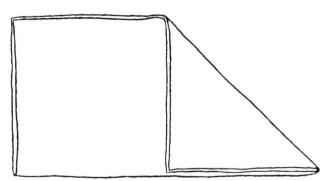

2. Holding your finger in the center of the top edge, fold the top right corner down to meet the center point of the bottom fold.

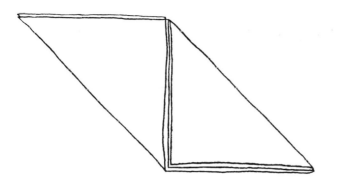

3. Holding your finger in the center of the bottom edge, bring the bottom left corner up to meet the top right corner.

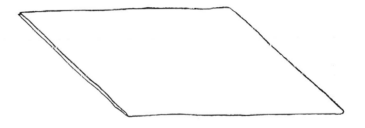

4. Holding the folds firmly in place, flip the napkin over.

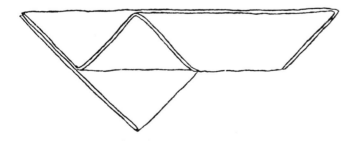

5. Grasping the center point of the long bottom edge, bring it up to meet the top edge. A triangle will be formed on the bottom.

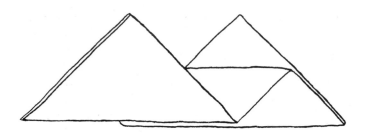

6. Holding the folds in place along the top edge, flip the napkin over once again. A second triangle will be formed. Both triangles should be pointing up.

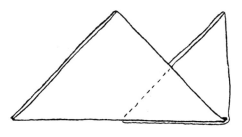

7. Take the right bottom corner and fold it toward the center, tucking the point all the way into the flap formed by the large triangle. The right side of the napkin should be completely straight. Turn the napkin over.

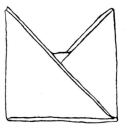

8. Repeat step 7 with the new bottom right corner, but do not turn the napkin over.

9. Holding the folds together, stand the napkin up and round out the center from the bottom so that it stands up well on its own. Stand the napkin up on the plate so that the crown faces the diner.

CROWN

Lotus

This gorgeous, four-sided flower design is best attempted after you've had a bit of folding experience. Use a large (at least 20 × 20-inch (50-by-50-centimeter)) napkin with a floral of geometric design.

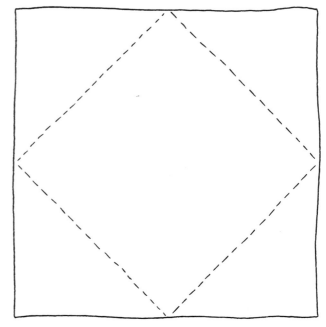

1. If the napkin has a right side and a wrong side, turn it wrong side up, and lay it flat down so that it is in a square before you.

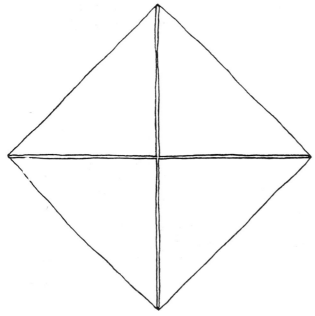

2. Fold the four corners in so that the points meet in the center. Adjust the napkin carefully so that all the new corners are sharp.

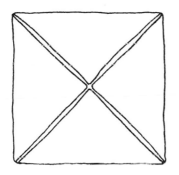

3. Next, fold the four new outside corners in, so that they also meet at the center.

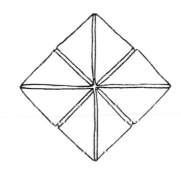

4. Holding the folds firmly in place, turn the napkin over, and repeat step 3.

5. Press down in the center with two fingers to hold the folds in place. With the other hand, lift each corner one at a time, pick it up, and sharply tug the loose point at the center of the back side outward. The folds should now stand up slightly. Place the napkin flat on the plate in a diamond or square shape.

LOTUS

BISHOP'S HAT

Bishop's Hat

This classic fold is fun to create and is not nearly as complicated as it looks. It works best with a starched napkin.

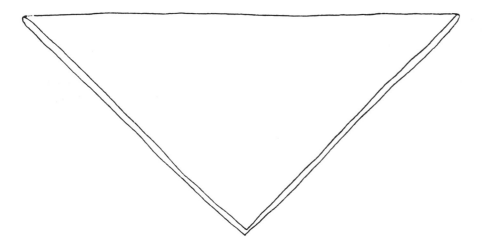

1. Fold the napkin in half to form a triangle with the point facing down, toward you.

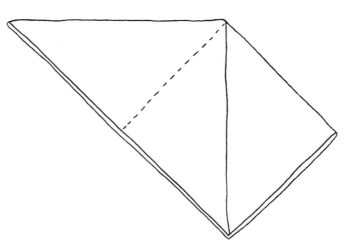

2. Holding your finger at the center point of the top fold, fold the right corner down to the bottom point.

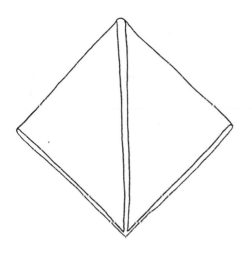

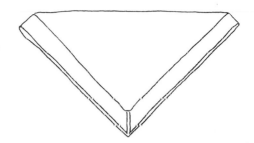

3. Repeat with left corner.

4. Bring the top point down to within 1 inch (2.5 centimeters) of the bottom point.

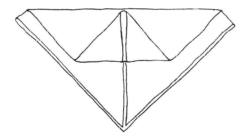

5. Fold the same point up to the center of the top edge.

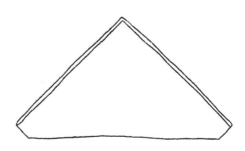

6. Holding the folds in place, flip the napkin over to the other side with the point facing up, away from you.

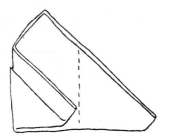

7. Fold the left corner to a little bit past the center point along the bottom edge.

8. Fold the right corner toward the center, and tuck the corner all the way inside the top flap of the fold made by the other side.

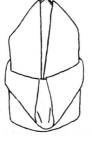

9. Holding the tucked-in fold together, stand the napkin up and round it out carefully so that it stands up on the plate with the decorative side facing the diner.

Variation

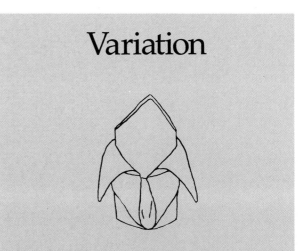

Repeat steps 1 through 9. Then gently pull the front top corners of the napkin down and out a bit like flower petals.

TWO-ROLL BASKET

Two-Roll Basket

This design is truly a showstopper. Fill the two sides of the "basket" with small dinner rolls, and place it toward or in the center of the table. Remember to use a lightly starched, very large damask or cotton napkin measuring at least 20×20 inches (50 by 50 centimeters).

1. Fold the napkin into thirds with the closed edge facing up. Crease your folds well after this and all other steps.

2. Fold the left side to meet the right side. The closed edge should be on the left.

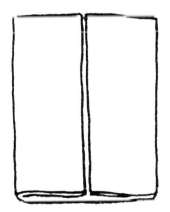

3. Then fold both new left and right sides in to meet at the center.

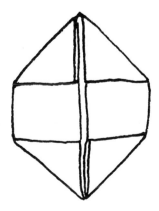

4. Fold down the top two corners to meet the center vertical line. Crease in place, and let the folds spring open again. Repeat with bottom two corners.

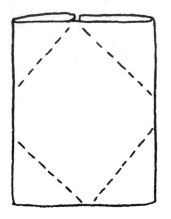

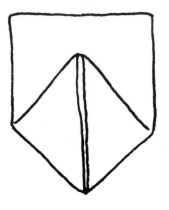

5. Turn the napkin over. You should see the four creases you just made.

6. Grasp the top two layers of the bottom edge at the center point of that edge. Lift those layers up to meet the center of the napkin and form a diamond.

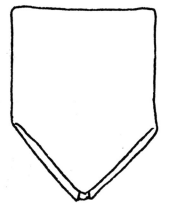

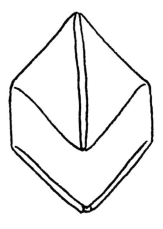

7. Fold the top point of the diamond down to meet the bottom point.

8. Grasp the top two layers of the top edge at the center point of that edge. Bring those layers down to meet the center vertical line and form a diamond. Leave this diamond open.

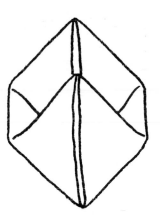

9. Open the bottom fold so that the diamond is exposed again and overlap this diamond with the top one.

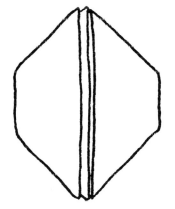

10. Turn the napkin over.

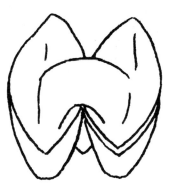

11. Open the left and right edges back and away from you. Standing the napkin up, spread out the long sides at the same time to create a double-sided basket.

Buffet Server

This design solves the problem of how to make sure guests at a buffet not only serve themselves food, but all the necessary silverware as well. Both napkin and silverware come together in one compact and attractive package that can be easily stacked.

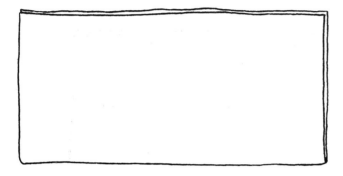

1. Fold the napkin up into a rectangle. The folded edge should be along the bottom.

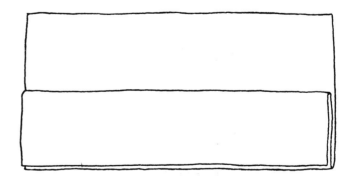

2. Bring the first layer of the edge down to meet the bottom edge. Turn the napkin over.

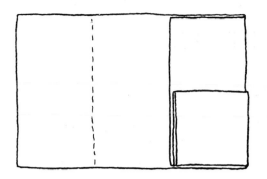

3. Fold the right edge to meet the center of the napkin.

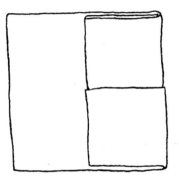

4. Fold the new right edge over again.

5. Repeat once more to create a rectangle with a pocket that can be filled with silverware and stacked or laid flat on a dinner plate.

BUFFET SERVER

TUXEDO FOLD

Tuxedo Fold

Reminiscent of a magnificent cumberbund, this design should be done with a starched napkin that will hold the crisp folds in place. Use your best white damask napkin for a formal look or a colored cotton one to make it more casual.

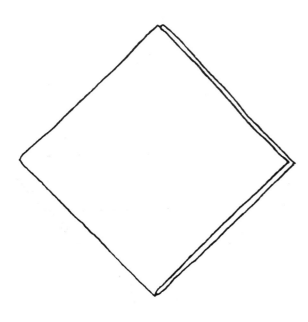

1. Fold the napkin into quarters, and place it in a diamond shape before you so that the closed corner is pointing down, toward you.

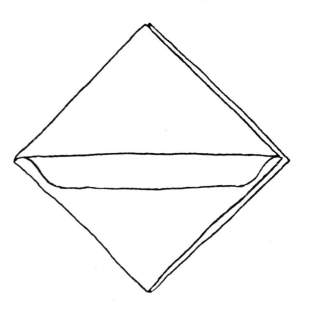

2. Roll the first layer of the top point down to the center line.

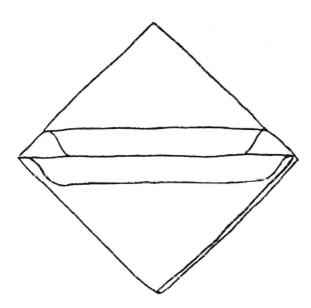

3. Gently lift that roll up, and fold over and tuck the point of the second layer part of the way down into the pocket behind the roll to create two bands of equal width.

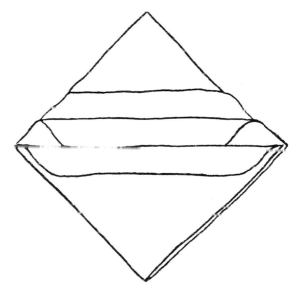

4. Fold the third layer down and behind the second to create a third band of equal width.

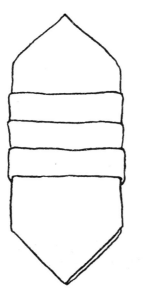

5. Fold the side points back and behind the napkin, overlapping them a bit in the back. Place the napkin on the dinner plate so that the points are vertical.

Variation 1

1. Repeat steps 1 through 4.

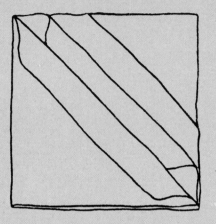 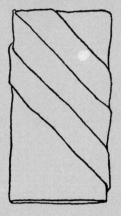

5. Rotate the napkin so that the last layer of the top point is now the upper right corner and the napkin forms a square before you.

6. Fold the left and right edges behind the napkin to form a rectangle. Place the napkin on the plate or beside it with the bands rising diagonally to the left.

Variation 2

1. Repeat steps 1 and 2.

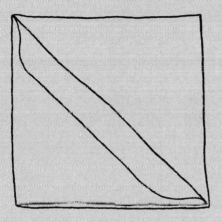 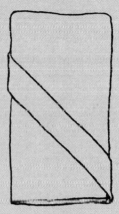

3. Rotate the napkin so that the roll runs on a diagonal from the top left to the bottom right.

4. Next fold the left and right edges behind the napkin to form a rectangle. Place the napkin on the plate so that the decorative band rises diagonally to the left.

Index

Basic Napkin Ring Fold, 32-33
Bishop's Hat, 93-96
Bouquet, 67-68
Bow Tie, 37-38
Breakfast Fold, 29-31
Buffet Server, 102-4
Bunny, 34-36

Candle Fold, 39-40
Candle wax stains, 15
Care of napkins, 11, 15-16
Carnation, 84-85
Catsup stains, 15
Centerpieces, 17
Children's parties, 17
Colors, 9
Cosmetics stains, 15
Cotton, 9, 13-14
Creases, 11, 12
Crown, 86-89

Dairy stains, 15
Deco Fold, 64-66
Dinners, napkins at, 9
Double Diamond, 44-45
Double Roll, 51-52
Dove, The, 71-72

Egg stains, 15
Envelope Purse, 20-23

Folding tips, 11-12
Folds
    Basic Napkin Ring Fold, 32-33

Bishop's Hat, 93-96
Bouquet, 67-68
Bow Tie, 37-38
Breakfast Fold 29-31
Buffet Server, 102-4
Bunny, 34-36
Candle Fold, 39-40
Carnation, 84-85
Crown, 86-89
Deco Fold, 64-66
Double Diamond, 44-45
Double Roll, 51-52
Dove, The, 71-72
Envelope Purse, 20-23
Lotus, 90-92
Love Knot, 78-80
Napkin Ring Fold, 32-33
Peacock's Tail, 61-63
Pineapple, 24-25
Pretty Points, 49-50
Ribboned Roll, 26-28
Roman Column, 46-48
Ruffle, 56-57
Seashell, 69-70
Shawl, 53-55
Shooting Star, 41-43
Split Square, 73-74
Triangle Blocks, 75-77
Tuxedo Fold, 105-9

Two-Color Picnic Pouch, 81-83
Two-Roll Basket, 97-101
Fruit stains, 15
Gravy stains, 15

Hems, 14
Holders, 12

Ice cream stains, 15
Ironing, 14
    damage during, 16

Lace, 13-14
Laundering, 11, 15-16
Linen, 9, 13-14
Lipstick stains, 15
Lotus, 90-92
Love Knot, 78-80

Materials, 13-14
Meat stains, 15
Milk stains, 15
Monograms, 14, 17
Mustard stains, 15

Napkin Ring Fold, 32-33
Napkin size, 11

Objects tucked in napkins, 17

Paper, 9, 13
Parties, napkins at, 9
Patterns, 9
Peacock's Tail, 61-63
Pineapple, 24-25
Placement, 12
Polyester, 12

Pressing, 14
    damage during, 16
Pretty Points, 49-50

Ribbon, 17
Ribboned Roll, 26-28
Roman Column, 46-48
Ruffle, 56-57
Seashell, 69-70
Selvages, 14
Shape of napkins, 12, 13
Shawl, 53-55
Shooting Star, 41-43
Soda stains, 15
Split Square, 73-74
Squareness of Napkins, 12,13
Stains, 15
Starching, 11, 14
Storage, 11, 12, 14
Surfaces for folding, 11

Tomato stains, 15
Top edge, location of, 11
Top point, location of, 11
Triangle Blocks, 58-60
Tri-Colored Triangle,75-77
Tuxedo Fold, 105-9
Twine, 17
Two-Color Picnic Pouch, 81-83
Two-Roll Basket, 97-101

Vegetable Stains, 15

Wine stains, 15